Defining Success
for the Small Church

by Michael P. Cavanaugh

ISBN 978-1-945423-32-1

For worldwide distribution
Printed in the USA

Table of Contents

Defining Success for the Small Church

After pastoring a church for 20 years, I became the full-time vice president of Elim Fellowship, the ministerial association I have been a part of since I graduated from Bible school. I wanted to be a help to the Elim Fellowship pastors, and I needed to have a clear sense of what they were facing, so I decided to visit the homes and ministries of as many pastors as I could.

Most of the churches they pastored were small churches. In one 18-month period, I visited about 100 pastors of churches that ranged in size from 25 to 100 people. Some of these churches were on the brink of dissolving, while others were filled with enthusiasm and fresh hope for the future. I was with some pastors who had been with the same congregation of 25 people for almost 40 years. I was with other pastors who worked full-time in a factory and still led a church of 75 people that had three services every week.

As I talked with these deeply committed, self-sacrificing spiritual warriors, my admiration grew and grew. These were people who plowed in hard fields, whose work was rarely celebrated, and who often faced criticism. I also realized that these pastors craved contact from their spiritual leaders, and they were moved by my expressions of interest, care and encouragement. It was this experience that birthed my desire to write this book.

How we define success for a church can have a profound impact on the self-esteem, confidence, and faith of a small church ministry team. If we define the win for small church leaders in such a way that it can never be attained — by relating it to large increases in attendance — we condemn those who are called to ministries that will never have large numbers to a life of frustration and self-doubt.

We have to recognize that large churches are not just small churches on steroids but are actually a different beast altogether. Comparing their measurements of success would be like comparing the success measurements of a mom-and-pop grocery store in an inner city with the success statistics of a big-box store in the suburbs. The managers of the big store would not even locate their store where the mom-and-pop store is, because it would not serve the purpose of what they are trying to accomplish and would limit their success as they would measure it. The big-box store is not just the mom-and-pop store grown big; it is another type of store altogether.

Large churches often have three key statistics that define them: the size of the attendance, the size of the offering, and the size of the buildings. These three statistics do give helpful information to the large church pastor, but they are not the total measurements of a healthy church.

Reality tells us that 75% of all churches have fewer than 150 people and that 50% of all churches have fewer than 75 people. I mention this because when you read stories of a person starting a church in their living room that then grows to 16,000 people over the next 10 years, it can be easy to ask the question, "What am I doing wrong?" The truth is God must really like small churches, because He has made a lot of them.

History tells us that the small church has been amazingly enduring through many cultural changes. As I'm writing this, our society is navigating the experience of the Covid-19 pandemic and the associated lockdown. Many large churches have huge buildings sitting empty, while small churches have continued to function as a caring community despite not being able to meet in person — because their community was never based on buildings or highly skilled performances but on mutual care. The large building of the church I formerly pastored for 20 years sits temporarily empty. I can remember when we built all 60,000 sq.

ft. of it, yet during a virus lockdown a large building doesn't help much.

So, the questions start to flood my mind. How do we define success in a small church? What roles do numbers play, including finances, attendance and building size? What is the definition of success for a church that is in a small rural community? What is the definition for success for a church targeting the inner-city? When can a small church celebrate? Can a church do well if it never grows numerically? It seems like so often instead of a small church being able to celebrate, there is this constant flood of disappointment —not quite meeting expectations, not quite accomplishing enough, not hearing the stories that you hear other people have about attendance growth.

I find many small church pastors can lose their way in terms of their vision for the church, because if they do not see results in terms of numbers, they feel ineffective. After trying several initiatives to grow the church population and failing, they give up — not just on numerical growth but also on improving and developing the church as a whole. They forget the many other ways that a healthy church is meant to develop, because all that seems to be measured is the numerical. Their sense of vision is destroyed because they are put in a no-win situation. Like a rat put in a maze where he can never find the food, the small church leadership just gives up trying.

Pastors who experience this level of discouragement often slip into simple maintenance mode. The leadership has become defeated because they have tried and failed repeatedly to find numerical success. Now they have given up on believing that the church can be anything special or that it can develop a unique contribution to the world. If they can't win the attendance, offering, or building game, they become convinced they can't win at all, and they lose their vision for development in almost every aspect of church life. Because it is not developing attendance growth, it is now not developing much in any area. You visit their church, and it seems stuck in a time warp.

My inspiration to write this book is a desire to help small church pastors re-envision what success is, so that they can have a sense of achievement, significance, accomplishment, fulfillment, and mission as they do Christ's work.

To avoid discouragement, it is important to focus our energy on what we can control rather than on what we can't control.

This is one of the big problems that I've observed in working with pastors of smaller churches: Their tendency is often to focus on things over which they have no power. I understand this because, even when my church got larger, I was not satisfied; I felt that we should be growing even more. I had to face this issue of always falling short of expectations in my own life. Was I going to live my ministry life under the weight of things I could not control?

For example, I can't control how many people will receive Christ, but I can control if we do three outreach events a year. I can't control people's responses, so I will be frustrated if I make that the measure of my success. I can't control if a person responds to Christ in the service, but I can control if I take time in the service to make room for a person to respond to the Lord. That is in my power.

I can't control what people decide to give to our church, but I can control if we teach on giving and provide people the opportunity to give. If the measure of my success is all wrapped up in what I can't control, then I feel powerless. I say to myself, "I've done everything I know to do. I've read every book I could put my hands on, but I'm not experiencing success."

Let me say this another way. Every church experiences decline each year. Between 6% to 10% of a church's attendance will be lost each year due to moving, death, backsliding, and people just wanting a change. This means that for a church to stay the same size, it must increase by 6% to 10% a year. Now every church also has a growth potential in their community, which is largely determined by the population around them. Eventually even growing churches reach the point where their growth potential and attrition rates match. This means that the growth potential of their area and the attrition rate they normally experience will match each other, and the church just can't grow any larger without a miracle of some kind happening.

This happened in the church I pastored. The church was located in a rural community. We were tremendously blessed and grew, especially in the beginning when we were smaller, but our natural growth potential was limited by the size of our community. Eventually we reached a point where our attrition rate and our growth potential were about equal. This meant that our overall attendance stayed the same, even though we worked very hard to keep growing each year.

Now you may be thinking that God can do a miracle and grow a church beyond its natural growth potential. I completely agree — but this is completely outside of our control. Why God does this sometimes but not others is one of those questions that I will have for Him in heaven. In the same way as I've seen some people miraculously healed and others not, it is a puzzle for me. I believe in the miraculous, but I can't control it. I pray for miracles every day, but until they come, I try to do the healthy things I know I should be doing no matter what.

So, our church's growth rate and our attrition rate became about equal, and the only way we could experience new growth would be to plant a satellite church in a new area that had its own growth potential. But it took me a long time to realize this, so I lived with a deep frustration for several years. *Why can't I get the church to grow? Why aren't I blessed like others? What is it about my leadership that is holding the church back? What demonic powers am I facing that others are not? Is my community somehow different? Am I not praying enough?* It is easy to think that numerical church growth is somehow rooted in the pastor's spirituality. *If God's anointing were heavy on me, the church would grow.* This thought tortured me for a long time.

How did I get over it? I began to realize that I knew some very godly, spiritual people who prayed more than I did and were better people than me, but their churches did not grow either. On the other side of the coin, I met a few leaders who had larger churches and yet seemed very spiritually immature to me. I finally surrendered the idea that my church's lack of growth was a measurement of my spirituality.

It dawned on me that I would lose heart and eventually give up if I kept focused on things I could not control. So I began to focus on activity that I believed would produce a healthy church — no matter what its size. I came to realize that ***developing a healthy church should be my definition of success.***

FOUNDATIONAL LEADERSHIP THOUGHT #1:

To Develop a Healthy Church Requires a Constantly Growing Pastor who is Fully Devoted to His Mission

Here are two key observations I've made:

1.   My first observation is that when leaders don't have a clear sense of what they should be working on, they have a tendency to float around "willy nilly" — doing the things that come easiest to them rather than continuing to personally develop. We don't develop because to grow you have to do something that you have never done before. If all my energy is going into working on the things that I have already mastered, it leads to stagnation in my personal development.

The ten areas of ministry I'm going to outline for you will give you a clear template of what you need to work on next in your church. This will force you to take on areas that don't come naturally to you, and you will be stretched. You will not be able to make ground in all ten areas at once. Instead, you will have a long-range plan of what needs to happen to cause your church to become healthy and flourishing. You will always have a "what's next" to focus on as you lead the church. When pastors don't know what they should be doing, they can consume a huge amount of time not doing anything productive. By having a plan that answers the question, "What's next?" you will always have something productive to focus on, and you will always be discovering new areas that you can grow personally in and that you can be encouraging your church to grow in.

2.   My second observation is that the greatest need in a small church is for a team-building leader, because there is no way just

one person can do all that needs to be done to grow a healthy church. Even if your family is heavily involved, you will still need more people. No matter how dedicated you are, there is no way you can do all that needs to be done without learning how to get other people involved.

Leadership is getting things done through other people, and I'll explain this concept in more detail. But first let me share with you another key leadership concept that will help you understand all that I'm sharing in the rest of this book.

FOUNDATIONAL LEADERSHIP THOUGHT #2:

To Develop a Healthy Church Requires an Understanding of the Value Zone Concept

Understanding the *value zone* concept helps you understand where the most important place is for you to put your time. The *value zone* is where the ministry of your church touches your people and community. Understanding your *value zone* will enable you to prioritize what the most important areas are that need your attention.

If I were to draw a circle on a whiteboard and call that first circle "the church," and then if I were to draw another circle that slightly overlapped the first circle and call it "people we serve," the area where those two circles overlap is called the *value zone*. Where the ministries of our church touch the people of the community that we are trying to serve — that is our *value zone*.

In a church, one of the times that is an extremely important time is Sunday morning. Why is it so important? It is the one time of the week that you touch the most people. You could sleep in all week long, have forgotten to make some important phone calls or missed a hospital visit, but if you have a good Sunday morning service, then 90% of the impact of that week will be accomplished. Why? Because that is where the most people are at the same time, that is where the contact is, that is where the connection is made with the most people. So, the *value zone* is where the church actually connects with people.

Now as a pastor you may have a lot of board meetings, but are they really in the *value zone*? It's not that you aren't discussing important things, but you never really touch anyone, connect with anyone, or link with anyone besides the few board members. Most people never really feel the benefit of those discussions.

Understand: These meetings are important, but they aren't really in the *value zone*.

Let me give you an example to which you may be able to relate. Imagine you're in a big-box store. The store has their motto written on the store wall in large letters: "Satisfaction is guaranteed." You're searching for an item that you can't find and after looking down several aisles, you realize you need help. You look around and see a young employee who is stacking cans on a shelf. He is probably the lowest paid person in the store. You go to him and ask, "Could you tell me where (item) is?" He stops, looks at you and frowns, and then says something like, "I have no idea. Maybe you could ask up front. I'm kind of busy right now."

The president of this big-box store and his board of corporate geniuses could be the greatest business minds in the whole world, but how do you feel about this store today? I'm thinking probably not so good. So, because that stock worker is in the *value zone*, he is the one who actually communicates everything about that store to you — all of the supposed values, slogans, and good will. All the ideals of the CEO and board only reach you through the lowest paid, least trained member of their staff. All their aspirations for their business have been placed in his hands to make it real to you.

Now instead, imagine if that young staff member had jumped up and said, "I'm not exactly sure where what you're looking for is, but let me see if I can help you find it." Then he walked with you for 5 minutes to the right section and helped you find just what you were looking for. How would you feel about that store now? Amazingly, the lowest paid, least trained person in the organization actually had more impact on your feelings about that store than the highest paid executive, because he is in the *value zone*. The job of a leader is to get the right people into the *value zone*, help them to realize that they are in the *value zone*, and give them the training they need to be successful at serving those whom they are trying to serve.

FOUNDATIONAL LEADERSHIP THOUGHT #3:

To Develop a Healthy Church, You Need to Understand the Definition of Leadership

A leader influences people to accomplish a purpose — this is the simplest and clearest definition of leadership I've personally ever been exposed to. I've found that it is critical to unpack what leadership really is because there are many misunderstandings attached to it. Often people think that leadership is some kind of mysterious force that some people are born with and others are not. But the truth is that leadership is exerted all the time in life, and it often has no prominent position attached to it.

For example, look at the definition again: "A leader influences people to accomplish a purpose." Let's take a mom who motivates her children to do their homework. She has influenced her children to accomplish the purpose of doing their homework. She is a leader.

I've found many people are so intimidated by the word leadership that I stopped using it in the church when I was trying to recruit people. If I asked people to *lead* a small group, they would say no — but if I asked them to *host* the group and *teach* the Bible study, they would say yes. If I asked them to *lead* the usher ministry, they would say no — but if I asked them to *coordinate* the usher ministry and *train* the ushers, they would say, "I can do that." There was so much intimidation around what a leader is that I found it was important for me to teach people exactly what leadership really means.

Often when I would hire someone at the church, one of my first talks with them was "the leadership talk." We might be at lunch together and I would grab a napkin and write this phrase on it: "Leaders influence people to accomplish a purpose." Then this phrase: "Doers just do the purpose." Then I would say something like this, "I can't afford to hire a *doer* — because if I hire a *doer*, all I get is their work. I need to hire a *leader* because *leaders* get other people to help do the purpose, not just themselves.

"For example, if I hire a *doer* worship leader, then I get one talented person who can put together a worship team and lead services. But if I hire a *leader* worship leader, I could get three teams providing opportunities for many musicians in the church to use their gifts. I also end up not overworking any of the teams, which gives everyone a more positive experience. I need you to be a *leader* if you're going to work here."

Pastor, you need to see yourself as a *leader* whose primary job is to get others to accomplish the purpose of ministry. I think this is what Paul was talking about when he said, "And He gave some as apostles, and some as prophets, and some as evangelists, and some as pastors and teachers, for the equipping of the saints for the work of service, to the building up of the body of Christ." (Ephesians 4:11-12 NASU) As a leader, your success is not measured by what you do; your success is measured by how many other people you have equipped and enabled to do God's purpose for His church. If you become just a *doer*, you will always have something to do, for sure, but you will never fulfill your destiny as a leader.

Your success as a leader is measured in how you have influenced other people to take up the mission of the church and give themselves in the accomplishment of it. I had it as a personal mission in my church that at least 50% of the people in the church had some job in the church on a weekly basis. This gave me a clear job to work on. It mobilized more people in ministry, it increased the interest and passion of those involved in the church, and it kept me focused on being a leader.

The *doer* job and the *leader* job are very different. They are both necessary for a church to function, but the church must be led by a *leader*. Imagine if you've been given the job of digging a ditch on the church property that is 50 feet long and 3 feet deep. A *doer* would say, "I need to be an example to everybody and get out there and dig. I'll invite others to join me, but if they don't, it doesn't matter. I'll get up early and stay up late, and if I keep working at it, eventually that ditch will be dug."

Leaders would think differently. They recognize that their job is not to dig the hole themselves but to get the job done by involving other people in the experience. And to do that, they will need to plan. First, they will define **what** they are doing, **why** they are doing it, **when** they need to have it done by, and **how much** the project will cost. Then they will think about **recruitment** of others to help. Maybe they can get 25 diggers, and they would need other people to help by keeping the diggers hydrated and to work on serving lunch after the dig. Then they would think about what **equipment** was necessary. They would need 25 shovels and supplies for carrying water and providing lunch. If they were experienced planners, they might try to think how they could make the experience fun by having a contest or having music playing in the background.

Because of this leader's work, maybe 35 people will have a part in accomplishing this project. They will feel a sense of ownership about the church whenever they remember that trench they were a part of building. They will also feel closer to the other people who worked side by side with them. The leader/ organizers may never lift a shovel full of dirt, but they would have gotten the mission accomplished through other people. The leader influences people to accomplish a purpose.

Sometimes we may have come from a home where all that mattered was your willingness to get in the hole and dig. You may have even been taught that a person who doesn't dig is really a shirker of responsibility. But this kind of thinking is totally wrong and will condemn you to never being able to be the leader you are needed to be.

Now as the leader, I should always be willing to climb in the hole and dig to get the job done. But if everything goes right, I won't have to because I've invested myself in getting the job done through others — and in the end, they will thank me for it because I gave them a great experience with new friends, a nice lunch, and even a few laughs.

Over my years as a pastor, as the church would grow, I had to change definitions of my job so that I could focus more on leading and less on doing. I didn't do this because I was trying to get out of anything, but because I realized that I had to give up to go up. I had to give up some area in which I had become a bottle neck so that I could focus on my job as a leader. This is one of the delicate balancing acts that a pastor has to navigate as their church grows. They need to constantly focus on the mission of "how can I get the most people involved in fulfilling the ministry of the church?"

I remember when I decided that I needed to focus more of my energy on preaching and leading, and I felt that I needed to get others involved in hospital visitation. We had a pastor dedicated to this kind of care and then we began training our small group leaders in how to visit people in the hospital. Before long, we had more people in our church visiting others than we had ever had. Just not me much anymore. I was now focusing more energy on getting others involved in the work of the ministry.

I remember when I decided that I needed to train more preachers in our church. I needed to give them a platform, so I began sharing my Sunday morning pulpit so they would have more opportunity. People loved seeing the developing young leaders taking up this role. Ultimately, when I stepped down as senior pastor, one of these young leaders took my place. A leader influences others to accomplish a purpose.

Something has to change in our thinking. As long as we are held prisoner by people's expectations or what an archaic job description says about the role of a pastor, we will never be released to do our real job of team building and getting others involved in the ministry. We need a brainwash to break free from ideas that have frozen us into a non-productive, non-affirming pattern for ministry, where we have no way of winning the game we are in. We can't blame this limited way of thinking on our church board or the expectations of others; we are limited by our own perspectives that are keeping us from being free to redefine the win in the church.

The win is to build a healthy church that is growing in the 10 areas of ministry I'm going to describe for you. It is not tied to other people's decisions, but rather to your personal decision to mobilize other people for ministry and build a team that is focused on doing ministry in the *value zone* of your church.

10 Areas of Development for a Healthy Church

I want to share with you 10 areas of development that can make your church healthy. I can't guarantee that if you focus on these areas that your church will grow big; there are just too many uncontrollable factors for me to make that promise. What I can guarantee is that if you focus on these development areas, your church will become healthier and stronger.

I believe God is worthy of our very best efforts. Malachi has some powerful things to say about us offering to God less than our best. Malachi 1:6-8 NASU: "'A son honors his father, and a servant his master. Then if I am a father, where is My honor? And if I am a master, where is My respect?' says the Lord of hosts to you, O priests who despise My name. But you say, 'How have we despised Your name?' You are presenting defiled food upon My altar. But you say, 'How have we defiled You?' In that you say, 'The table of the Lord is to be despised.' But when you present the blind for sacrifice, is it not evil? And when you present the lame and sick, is it not evil?"

God is offended by an effort that is less than our very best. He is not looking for perfection; He is looking for the honoring that comes with our presenting to Him the best that we have. If we as pastors allow ourselves to be choked out by discouragement and destined for failure, we become defeated, and we cannot muster the energy or enthusiasm to give God our best. So, we need to come to the place where we stop looking for the affirmation of large attendance and instead feel the inspiration that comes from knowing we are giving to God the best that we have to offer.

Finally, before you can embrace these 10 areas of development, you must also answer the question, "Is God put off by my planning and organizing work?" I know this sounds strange, but I've found that many church leaders hold a secret suspicion that God doesn't really like us to plan, that somehow our effort steals glory from Him and represents a lack of trust in Him. We fear that our planning will box God in and limit what He can do. Now, we normally don't have these same ideas about our personal lives. We believe in planning for our first house, to replace our car, or for retirement — but we think that somehow the church should be healthy and strong without any planning.

There is no question that there are Biblical examples of people who trusted in themselves and their own ability above God — and they were rebuked for it. However, there are also examples of leaders who planned and organized — and they were in the center of God's will. Nehemiah and Joseph are two who come to mind.

To embrace the areas of development about which I want to talk with you, you must first believe that God is honored by your efforts to think through what you're doing for Him. He is also honored when you try to do the very best of your ability to evaluate and improve on your efforts. As you do this, not only will you get better and better in what you're doing for Him, but He will be honored by your intentionality.

If you will focus on the development areas that I lay out for you in this book, I believe you will experience the fruit of improvement, the satisfaction of accomplishment, and the sense that your offering is pleasing to God because it is composed of your best effort.

CHURCH DEVELOPMENT AREA #1 —

The Sunday Morning Service

An effective Sunday morning service takes preparation and planning; it is in the *value zone* of your church. More people are directly affected by the Sunday morning gathering than anything else you do. Before you consider putting together a team to do a summer Vacation Bible School or a Christmas program, you should put together a team to have the best Sunday experience possible.

The thing I want you to get a hold of is that most of the time in churches, especially in small churches, the church is attempting to do too much overall. The church needs to do less overall. Now that doesn't sound right, does it? Church wisdom might say, "We need to have more ministries. We need to have more ministries happening to appeal to more people." But the reality is that if your church is doing too much, this leads to your best volunteers being overworked, mediocrity in what ministries you do have, and a lack of clarity about what you are actually wanting to accomplish.

I remember when I came to this realization in my own church. For years we had put on magnificent Christmas programs. We would have 200 or more volunteers involved in making it happen. People were involved in creating, planning, rehearsing, set design, and promotion; the list would go on and on. It took many months of effort for us to pull it off. People would come from miles around to see it, and I have many warm memories of the effective outreach ministry that happened each year at Christmas.

But there was a problem. We had a fabulous Christmas program which occurred once a year, but our normal Sunday morning service which occurred weekly was mediocre. In comparison to the Christmas program, it felt thrown together. Nobody really thought about it in advance, nobody rehearsed complicated parts of the meeting, nobody thought about how we could make transitions better, nobody was thinking about how we could add media or even skits to communicate the sermons better, and there was no evaluation process each week to determine how we could improve.

I started wondering why we didn't have the same spirit of excellence in our Sunday morning service as we did in our Christmas production. I realized that one of the big reasons was that most of our best people were already deeply committed to our annual Christmas production. There was no way we had the manpower or energy to do both well.

Here is where the *value zone* comes in. Which activity was more in the *value zone* — the once a year, weekend long Christmas performance or our weekly church services? It was clear to me that more people would benefit if we could raise the excellence of our weekly services. You need to understand me here; I'm not against Christmas productions. Ours was awesome and I later started doing it again, but not until I had raised the level of excellence of the weekly services which were much more in the value zone.

Let me give you several areas to focus on when thinking about the Sunday morning experience. You might need to develop teams in several of these areas. Remember, a leader gets things done through other people.

When you are trying to bring fresh vitality to a ministry, it does not require a huge expenditure of money. Many things that can be done are what I refer to as low-hanging fruit. They are small things that have a big impact. Making changes in a few visible but often neglected areas can give you a big boost in momentum.

If you can have one success even in a small area, it can give you the foothold you need try in another area. When a string of these small successes is put together, you get the hope and momentum for larger changes. Often when we are trying to introduce change, we have a tendency to think that we need to do something big and dramatic, but actually change most often begins with small things that create hope and inspire people to put out the effort to see bigger changes.

Cleanness and Freshness of Facility — This is so basic that it is often ignored. Stand on the outside of your building from where a visitor will enter. What do you see? Does the landscaping look neglected? Is the paint around the door and windows peeling? Is the front door sagging and broken? They speak of neglect and a lack of care. You may not have much money to spend, but these areas don't need money — they need love. A team of men and women could make the building look tremendously loved in six Saturday mornings a year. It would take a leader and the wholehearted support of the pastor, but for very little investment of money the outside of the church could get a great face-lift.

What about the bathrooms in the church? If I told you that I could get a quick assessment of the character of the leaders of a church by visiting the church's bathroom, what would you think? What would your church's bathrooms say about you today? Are they freshly painted? Are there holes in the wall board from some half-finished plumbing project? Is there rust around metal fixtures? None of this requires a lot of money. There is no need to replace everything with new stuff at this point. What you're looking for is that feeling that the place is valued and cared about. It is the same feeling that you get when going into the home of a person who does not have a lot of money, but who cares for what they do have; you can't help but admire that. A lot of times we cannot control our income level, but we can control how we treat what we have. I don't have to be rich to make my home inviting. I just have to care.

When I first started in ministry, I was the assistant pastor in a small church in upstate NY. The church was struggling, and the attendance was getting so low that it might become non-viable. In order to not overwhelm the finances of the church, the lead pastor had a job as a school bus driver, and I was not being paid at all. One day the lead pastor and I were praying about what we could do to help the church. As we were praying, I felt the Lord speak to me, "First the natural, then the spiritual." What?! That didn't sound right. It was a church after all. But I could not escape the clarity of the word placed in my heart. What did it mean?

As I was sitting in the church sanctuary, I looked up and saw that all eight of the main lights hanging down in the sanctuary had large white globes over them, except one. The globe on that one was literally shattered and only half of it was still attached to the light fixture. As I stared at it, I thought to myself, "How have I never noticed this before? That light does not even look safe. What if the remainder of the globe fell on someone?" I pointed it out to the pastor and we both were shocked. I committed to repair it, and that week I went to a light fixture store and bought with my own money a new glass globe that very nearly matched all the others. I found a ladder and replaced it.

When I replaced it, it felt like my eyes were suddenly opened. I looked around the church and I could see things with different eyes. I noticed that all the windowsills were filled with dust and dead flies. I could see supplies piled up in corners of the room we were worshipping in. I had been blind to all of this disorder and uncleanliness. We began to tackle all this stuff — and people began to feel the difference. They had grown used to the dirt and neglect, but now they could feel the care and love. Their self-esteem went up, because they could feel that their church was loved and cared for — and visitors began to come. The Lord had to show us that our problem was not a spiritual one; it was a natural one.

Comfortable Seating — Seating can be a problem. It can be expensive, but the simple truth is that the "mind can only receive what the seat can endure." Here is a helpful tip for you: Often megachurches and colleges have older seating that no longer meets their needs, and they would be happy to donate to you or possibly sell to you for pennies on the dollar. Knock on a few doors; you may be shocked at what is available that will perfectly meet your need. I've literally had hundreds of thousands of dollars of forgotten furniture donated to ministries I've led. It can be a real boost when an amazing donation of newer-than-what-you-currently-have chairs are brought into a room in your church.

Sound and Media Tech — Tech people always want the latest and greatest equipment, but they will also scour Craigslist or Facebook Marketplace to find it. Adding equipment in this area will be a great encouragement to your sound and media team and make your presentations even better. I've found that these tech folks desperately want to use their gifts for God and will spend countless hours trying to improve the church's presentation — if you will show an interest in what they are trying to accomplish. This area needs more investment now than in the past because American society has put so much emphasis on quality technical presentations. You don't have to try and compete with a megachurch that has multiple staff dedicated to just sound and media production, but you can try to add some media into what you do. It will require you as the leader to grow in a new area and possibly to plan further ahead so that others have the ability to try and help you; I'll talk more about this idea later.

Digital Church Services — As a result of the Covid-19 pandemic, all churches now need to have a way to broadcast their services online. Remember, less is more. If you can't make a strong musical presentation, get help from those who can. When I was doing the chapel services on Zoom for the Bible college I led, I didn't feel we had the technical strength to do strong musical presentations on that platform. So I went to YouTube and simply started the Zoom chapels sharing my screen and streaming a high-quality worship ministry for the first 10 minutes. It was not as strong as worship in person, but I was shocked at how effective and well-presented it came across. Using Zoom combined with YouTube and little to no money, you can have digital church.

Facebook offers many options for broadcasting, also. You can do this.

Service Evaluation — It is not wrong to take the time to have a team evaluate your Sunday services. Have the team members who do the evaluation also be the ones who work on fixing the problems.

For example, maybe you have an old goose-neck microphone stand. When people of different heights come to the mic, they adjust it by moving it up or down or to the side, (goose-neck stands are flexible), but every time it moves, it groans or screams. This can be quite annoying when it happens every week. Who is going to lubricate the stand or work with the sound team to get something different for the job?

How about transitions in the service? How can we improve them? Is there a way we could do announcements without having people stand up in the congregation to shout them out? Could we have a system where announcements are planned in advance? No one is going to ask these questions of how to make things better unless they are given permission by the pastor and have a clear plan to do at least one thing each week to make Sunday morning better.

Every time a change is made it needs to be celebrated. These are your little wins that build momentum and hope. I can't control if my church is going to have a huge spurt in growth, but I can control whether the windowsills are clean or the goose-neck mic stand has been replaced. Celebrate the people who make each of these changes possible.

How do you celebrate people? It is simply saying thank you as sincerely and publicly as you can. Why publicly? When you thank people publicly, you not only give the gift of gratitude to a well-deserving person, you also model for everyone what being a servant looks like. What gets recognized gets repeated; it is that simple. So, share it from the pulpit, have a party, mention it in the bulletin, use it as a sermon illustration. Just be sure to celebrate the things that get accomplished. It generates momentum.

Effective Children's Ministry — Your children's area has to be absolutely outstanding. It needs to be cleaner than clean and fresher than fresh. I've found that parents will go to a church they only marginally like if they know that their kids are well taken care of.

Do everything you can to make parents feel their kids are in a safe environment. First, make sure your workers are screened. There are services that will do background checks for $25 or less.

Also, make sure the building is prepared and safe for kids. I've been shocked to walk down a church's hall leading to the children's area and see open storage shelves filled with cleaning and painting supplies. Parents need to know their kids are in both a personally and physically safe environment.

Get a team of fanatics working on your children's area. You can make this better than you have ever had before. Don't have many children yet? No problem. Make the kids you do have celebrities and go above and beyond for them. I'll bet God will give you more.

When I was a pastor, I tried on Sunday mornings to repeatedly communicate my value for children. I would say something like this: "As you're listening to me this morning, you may be thinking that we want to entertain your children while we teach you adults. The truth is just the opposite: I'm trying to keep you entertained while we have a chance to teach and impart to your children. As adults, you have already messed up half of your lives, but when we win a child, we get their whole life dedicated to God." Now I said this half joking, but the truth is that we did have that kind of value in our hearts when thinking about their children, and the parents deeply appreciated it.

Parents are searching for help. You don't have to be big or rich to love their children. It is something that you have the power to do.

Advanced Sermon Planning — When I first began in the ministry, I would plan my sermons on a weekly basis. Every Monday, I would begin the week wondering what I was going to teach on that next Sunday. I felt this was necessary to hear the Lord for that week; I wanted my sermon to be a fresh word from God. I'm not sure why I thought the Lord didn't know what was going to be needed a month or even a year from now, but somehow I thought that it would be better to hear what God wanted to say this week during the week itself.

There are a lot of problems with this kind of thinking. For one, it limited the research I could do to prepare for my message, because it would take me half the week to figure out what I was going to talk about, so that left only a short amount of time to do research.

The other big problem is that if I don't know what I'm talking about until the Wednesday before Sunday, then it severely limits my ability to get help from other people involved in the preaching process. How could I give time for the worship leader to pick a song that related to my topic when I only knew a day or two before what the topic was? How could people who had interest in drama help me to communicate if they had no time to find good material or rehearse? How could people who might be willing to decorate the church for a given theme have time to do that if I didn't know what my theme was until Thursday? How could the media team prepare PowerPoints or film clips in such a short time? I think you get the point. I realized that if I wanted to involve other people in the preaching ministry process, I would need to plan at least a month in advance. Amazingly, I discovered that even when I prepared my sermon topics in advance, God still knew what needed to be said and there was still a prophetic touch on the sermons — except now many more people could help me to make the best impact possible.

You may be asking yourself, "Why he is so worked up about involving other people?" Remember, the leader influences people to accomplish the purpose, while the doer just does the purpose. Our job as leaders is equipping the church to do ministry. The more people we involve in the process of doing ministry, whether it is cleaning, painting, sound, evaluation, children's ministry or a Facebook broadcast, the more we are succeeding in our mission.

A much more important measurement to me than how many people might attend your church each week is how many of those who attend are involved in the ministry of the church on a regular basis. If I can get at least 50% of the people involved in ministry, I'm winning big time and so is the kingdom of God. In a rural area, or an oppressed urban area, I will never have a huge attendance, but I can get those who are with me involved in the ministry — especially if I have a clear vision of what needs to get done.

You may be thinking to yourself, "This guy doesn't understand what I'm going through. I only have ten people in my church, and I work a job on top of my pastoral ministry." If that's you, the first thing I would do is sit down with at least half the people and ask this question: "What one thing are we capable of doing, that would be most in the value zone and would affect the most people positively for Christ and our church?" Then begin working on that one thing as a team. You don't try to do everything; you try to do one thing and get a win under your belt as a team. Maybe your one thing is to find a building to meet in. Maybe it is to invite people to a small group event. Maybe it is to paint the front door of the church. I have no idea of your specifics, but the key is to define your next step, complete it, and then say, "We were able to do that! What one more thing could we do next?" Let the wins build up, let the momentum build up, and let the sense of empowerment fill your hearts.

CHURCH DEVELOPMENT AREA #2 —

Effective Care

How can you improve the care that your people receive? How have the processes of care changed in your church in the last 10 years? How have you involved other people in the care process?

Sometimes people think that the pastor is the only one who should do care in the church, but remember that you want to do these jobs through people you have trained.

It is very important that when you are training people in the pastoral care area of your church, they see themselves as your representative. They need to keep you posted on what is happening in the lives of the people they are touching, and they need to always see themselves as your hand extended to the hurting in the congregation. The idea is that you would like to be with everyone but you as one person can't do the best job for everyone, so you have brought them into the process to help you. They represent you. Encourage them to always begin their visits saying something like, "Pastor was concerned about you, and he asked about you and if I would visit you on his behalf. Is there anything I can pray with you about? Is there anything you would want me to make sure he knows?"

One time I was working with a volunteer in youth leadership, and I was concerned about how a certain young person was doing. So I asked the youth leader about that young person and he responded, "Pastor, I can't talk to you about this young person because they have spoken to me in confidence." This created a real problem because it was like my hand stopped talking to my brain. How could I make sure the young person under my charge was receiving the proper care, if the worker I had put with them would no longer talk to me? I tried to explain that, as my representative, he could not give anyone complete confidentiality. Everyone needed to understand that the youth worker was my representative and that if they spoke to the youth worker it was like speaking to me. The youth worker saw himself like an independent agent and as a result felt that this young person was exclusively his responsibility. I had to remove him from the position.

Fortunately, this was the only time I had a problem like this, but it taught me something important: I needed to make clear to those in the care realm how important it was that they not get between me and the flock but that they be my representative to the flock.

Hospital Visitation — All of us do some of our jobs by role and other jobs by gifting; we are most effective when we are most aligned with our gifts. There are people who are gifted in care and then there are people who are willing. I try to get the gifted people doing what they are good at. Get compassionate, empathetic people involved in care ministry. Form a team and give them periodic training in how to be a help to people in crisis.

What creative things could you and your team do to make hospital visitation better?

Small Groups — This can be a wonderful area of ministry. Small groups can strengthen friendships, discipleship, and participation in the church.

There are so many different ways to make this ministry work for your church. Groups can be long-term or only run for a few weeks. Groups can be Bible study-based or affinity-based around a common interest (like motorcycles) or common life stage (like young mothers). Groups can focus on education or relationships. Groups can be a backbone of your church's programming with very high levels of participation, or a side emphasis for only those interested. Let your team's creativity flow; think how you can use groups to make your church experience better. Experiment and find what will work for your people.

Wedding Support — There is so much involved in putting together a wedding. How is your premarital counseling handled? Is there a way you could involve other people, like possibly having a mature couple who get trained in using a set of premarital counseling videos combined with some meaningful conversations? How could you support people who are doing weddings in your little church? Is there someone who would love to be your church's wedding planner?

I'm not saying that pastors can't do all these jobs themselves or that they should not keep some parts of the process exclusively for them as the pastor, but our job is to train others to do what we do. There are gifted people in your church who would be totally ignited by the chance to help a young couple get a good start.

Funeral Support — Funerals are a critical time when a pastor can really bond with a family. But there are so many parts to the process that a funeral team — people who understand how to work with the local undertakers, who can provide a nice meal at the church, or who can do some follow-up visits after the funeral — can be exceptional support to the pastor. What has your church done to improve your funeral support in the last 5 years? Have you even evaluated how things have gone?

Special Needs Support — Every church will find itself facing some unique special needs; disabilities abound and so do the needs that face churches. It could be a wheelchair-bound individual, an ADHD child, or visitors from the local group home. Small churches can't usually help in all these situations, but I've found that God is faithful to connect you with a special need that touches your church family. No pastor can be an expert in all these areas, but as God gives you access to human and financial resources, you can tackle some of these different areas. How about putting together a team to study how your church could be exemplary in relating to that special need?

Counseling Support — As a pastor, I observed five different kinds of counseling opportunities that commonly present themselves.

First, was the single visit, the "I need to talk through a problem or challenge that I'm facing so I can make a good decision" kind of counseling.

Second, was the "I need someone in my life to disciple me" kind of counseling. This is a cry for friendship and mentoring.

The third kind of counseling was relational family counseling. Some of this could be addressed simply by someone who has been further down the road than the person being counseled. At other times it called for a professional counselor who could walk someone through deep family dysfunction.

The fourth kind of counseling was focused on spiritual deliverance from demonic forces that were working to hinder a person's life development.

The fifth kind of counseling was professional counseling for mental health issues that would likely require medication and supervision.

As a pastor, I would meet with anyone one time. During that meeting, I would assess the depth of a person's need, and I tried to know of resources that could help them wherever on this spectrum they found themselves: groups that could mentor, professional counselors who would honor a person's spiritual life, intercessors who would pray and oppose demonic oppression, family counselors who could help people think clearly in current relationship conflicts, and people who could help navigate the social services and the local mental health options.

After meeting with someone, I would help the person connect with whatever resources I felt would be the greatest help for them. Rarely, I might meet with someone 4 or 5 times if I felt I had something special to contribute to them. But I never presented myself as a professional counselor, because I honestly have neither the training nor temperament for that job. The amount of effort involved in putting together these resources is incredible. Wouldn't it be great to form a team who could identify and promote these kinds of resources to help people? You might not be able do this all by yourself, but a team could do it and they could update these resources.

Each of these situations offers opportunities to involve compassionate, care-giving members of your church who would be forever grateful that you helped them find a way to help others.

<u>Church Management Software</u> – Do you think your church might benefit from church management software? This can help the church with everything like finances, communication, coordination of events and even turn peoples' cell phones into part of their church experience. This is part of a family of software called Customer Relationship Management or CRM. Just put "church management software" into Google and stand back. You may be amazed at some of the very affordable options available to you that can add a touch of digital relevance to a small church that has been around a long time.

CHURCH DEVELOPMENT AREA #3 —

The Connecting Process

How do you help people move from visiting the church to being active members of the church? Healthy churches see an average of 1 in 4 visitors stay in the church. How do you encourage visitors to return to and become a part your church?

How Do You Track Guests? What system do you have for collecting key follow-up information from a person who visits your church? This could be as simple as having someone go to them personally after the service and ask them to fill out a card, or having a number the person can text to and give you their information via text. The key is that you need to have some way of getting key contact information from every visitor you have. This is essential and must not be left to chance.

How Do You Invite Them Back? How will you make clear to guests that they are welcome, and you want them to come again? Could someone call and welcome them? Could you send them a letter after their first visit? Would you want someone to visit them? Could you send them a gift? I'm not telling you what to do; I'm simply saying that you and your team need to decide what you are going to do.

Why is having them come back for a second visit so important? Because if they do, there is a 50% chance they will then keep coming to your church. If I told you that there was a group of people who, if you just connected to them in some way, there would be a 50% chance they would regularly attend your church, I bet you would think that was a very valuable contact and worth every effort. Your guests are exactly this, which is why you must have a thought-out process for making your love felt by them.

<u>When They Come Back, What Is the Next Step for Them?</u> Think about this term "next step." People often struggle making big commitments, so one of the ways we can help them is by breaking a bigger commitment down to a series of smaller steps. If I asked a person if they would want to join my church, they might struggle with making that commitment. But if I invited them to a pizza lunch after church to meet the pastor, they might easily say yes. If I sent them an email with a brief video clip of the pastor inviting them to the pizza lunch, that might be even better. Why? Because hitting a link is even simpler than going to lunch; it might be a perfect next small step.

You need to make sure that you can always answer the question for someone concerning what they should do next in their journey at the church. This can be communicated in personal conversation, a phone call, an email or a video clip. The key is that your team has thought through what they want a person who has visited the church one time — or visited the church a second time, or taken an introductory video class on the website, or attended a welcome lunch, or asked how they might serve in the church — to do next. This can be very simple and personal when the church is small, but it must be followed up on. People who visit your church are just too valuable to be ignored, and their destinies may literally hang in the balance.

CHURCH DEVELOPMENT AREA #4 —

Stewardship

Stewardship is the process of teaching people that their time, talents and treasures belong to God. This includes how you motivate givers and train people in personal financial management. Godly money management is essential to personal growth and Kingdom growth.

Healthy Thinking About Money — In my 20 years as a pastor, I learned several key lessons about money that I would like to share with you.

Money Lesson 1 was just **_how important personal money management is to a person's success in life._** If I trained a young family in good money management, I greatly reduced the destructive pressure on their marriage and helped set them up for success in life. The lessons I taught on money were often seen as some of the most practically impacting that people received at church, and they would always thank me for getting them on the right road. I did this in many ways, including teaching an annual sermon series on finances and leading small groups and classes on the subject. Dave Ramsey's video teachings always made a great class for the church; when people learn how to avoid debt and become debt-free, it changes so much for them.

Money Lesson 2 was that **_me knowing the giving of those in our church was a great help to me in pastoring them._** It would give me great insights into the spiritual condition of my flock. I heard John Maxwell say, "The last thing to come to church is a person's wallet and the first thing to leave is their wallet."

If someone who gave regularly to the church had stopped giving, the financial secretary of the church would inform me. I wanted to know not because I wanted to scold them, but because it was evident that something was happening in their lives. I would call them and ask them how they were doing. Often I would discover that the family was facing some kind of personal financial calamity that the church was able to help with, or that they were suffering a health struggle, or that they had taken up an offense about something and were on the verge of leaving the church. My awareness of the change in their financial giving helped me to connect with them in a time of spiritual or physical need.

Some leaders say that the pastor should not know their congregation's giving because it would cause the pastor to practice favoritism. This was not my experience; instead, I was able to use the information to better care for my flock. Some people who have a spiritual gift of giving express their service to the church primarily through finances, while others give time by volunteering. When we were facing different kinds of financial challenges, it helped me to know who the time volunteer givers were and who the financial givers were.

Knowing the giving in the church also gave me discernment into people's motivations during times of difficulty. When I was new to the pastoring of my church, there were two men who were very visible to the church and who would often try to exert pressure on me in the direction they felt the church should go. As a young pastor, I very much wanted to please these men; I wanted their approval. I remember one particular time when I was trying to exert some leadership in the church and was speaking at a men's group. When I would say things with which they agreed, they would visibly nod their heads up and down, but if I said something with which they did not agree, they would visibly shake their heads from side to side. This was very disturbing to me as I tried to lead, and my heart was tied in knots as I tried to figure out how to please them.

The next week, quite by accident, I came across their church giving records. I was shocked; neither of them had given anything to the church in several years. Here I was stressing myself trying to please two people who were not really on board with the church in this most practical way. Knowing this information enabled me to put their approval in perspective.

Stewardship of personal finances and time management is critically important to the success of any church — or life, for that matter. The church needs an intentional plan for developing people in this critical area. It will help your followers to be personally successful, and it will release finances for the church also.

Money Lesson 3 that I learned was **the value of principled giving above emotional giving.** Principled giving is when people give because of a principle that they believe. Emotional giving comes when a person's heart is touched in some way and they give in response to that emotional tug. Some church people have been trained to give only when their heart strings get tugged. This means that the pastor must come up with a moving story every week just to cover the normal operational expenses of the church. It increases the temptation to manipulate people's emotions, and I could not function like this. Once principled giving is established in the church, there is no need to have to manipulate people emotionally and the pressure is off you.

In our church, I would take a month almost every year to teach on personal financial management, debt-free living, and honoring God with the first-fruits tithe of all that is received. You will have given them the tools that they need in their own lives to succeed financially. There is still the occasional moving story that people will respond to, but there is no pressure to manipulate.

Annual Stewardship Sermon Series — As I just mentioned, I found this to be a critically important tool for developing people and for developing the church. January is a good time to do this series, because people are wanting to make fresh commitments to make their upcoming year better. I would challenge them about things like getting out of debt personally or beginning a system for saving in their personal lives. I would also usually end each series giving people a chance to commit to tithing for the coming year.

Recurring Financial Management Class — Offering a class that starts soon after you finish your stewardship series is a great way to help people follow through on their desire to get their finances under control. Over the years, I've had many people tell me that our church's teaching was the key to their financial success and that they never would have owned a home if we had not taught them how to manage their money. Nothing could be more practical for them or the church than teaching on this incredibly valuable life skill.

Leadership Accountability — Because we taught the principle of tithing, which we defined as giving the first 10% of your income to the Lord, all our church's key leaders committed to be an example in that area by honoring the Lord with the tithe. We just felt that we could not ask others to do this if we in the leadership were not examples in this area. Each year as they recommitted to the areas of leadership they led, we asked them to recommit to tithing.

CHURCH DEVELOPMENT AREA #5 —

Volunteer Development

Healthy churches have at least 50% of their people with some ministry involvement. Volunteer involvement is key to personal spiritual growth and to the advancement of the kingdom. How do you move people into ministry in the church?

<u>Annual Volunteer Recruitment Sermon Series</u> — There are some key issues in a church that are too important to leave to chance, and people need to be brought back to them again and again. Stewardship is one important issue that I just mentioned, but teaching people about our calling to serve Christ and the people He loves is another one of them. On an annual basis I would do a series on serving and volunteering. As the old saying goes, repetition is the mother of learning. These principles that are so central to the Bible's teaching need to be reemphasized, especially in this sin-sick world in which we live.

The Bible says in Mark 16:20, "And they went out and preached everywhere, while the Lord worked with them, and confirmed the word by the signs that followed." This passage is referring to the way that, when they preached the Word, there were miracles that occurred to show that what was preached was from God. I've come to see this principle to also work in another way. If I want to see the people of the church become faithful in their financial management, I need to preach about finances and then God will confirm the word with signs following in that area. If I want the people to be faithful in the use of their time in service to others, I need to preach about serving and volunteering. When I do this, God will confirm the word with signs following and people will grow in this area. Nothing just happens by accident in the church. As the pastor, I need to build into the church through preaching and personal example the model of what I want them to become.

This is why there are several of these ten development principles that I teach on every year.

Spiritual Gift Identification Class — A great class to have ready to begin when you finish your series on serving is a spiritual gift identification class. Helping people to identify their spiritual gifts is a great way to help them find an avenue of service that matches who they are. People will always be more motivated and more effective if they are serving in the area of their gifting. Everyone understands that you can't be 100% in your area of gifting all of the time; some jobs we do because they are needed, or our role demands that we do them. But if we can help people find their gifts, they will be forever grateful. Classes like these can be run every year, because there are always a handful of people who have not taken them before. There are several classes that you can get on video if you do a little research.

Appreciation Events — Saying thank you is one of the simplest, most basic things that you can do. The importance of gratitude is all over the Bible, but amazingly in churches it is often neglected. You should have an annual event that is built around saying thank you to all your volunteers. Every church has people who like to organize parties; get them in a room and let them plan and implement a thank you event every year. You will not regret it.

Burnout Avoidance Plans — Many churches work like this: Someone is asked if they will teach a children's class and they say yes — but we never talk to them about the class again for a decade, even to say thank you. I think the fear is that if we talk to them, they will want to quit. So instead, we ignore them. How about getting a team of people together to talk about how to help people avoid burnout in their ministry? In our church we started giving all teachers six weeks off during the summer by recruiting a special 6-week summer team to cover their classes. You may have a different approach, but what are you doing to help your workers avoid burnout? How are you removing the stigma that if someone says yes to a job in the church, they are stuck in that job forever?

You may not have a larger church this year, but wouldn't it be an incredible win if you developed a plan for avoiding burnout for your children's workers? Things are better here than they were before. You can put a star in the win column, and it's better because you brought leadership to the church that you pastor.

CHURCH DEVELOPMENT AREA #6 —

People Development

How do you stimulate growth in your people's spiritual lives? How do you make disciples at your church? If someone has been at your church for five years, how are they a better person as a result? How do you help people have power encounters with God? What value has been added to their lives as a result of being in your church?

Your church may or may not be growing in terms of attendance, finances and building, but are your people growing? There are many ways to do this. Small groups with a teaching emphasis, traditional Sunday school, Sunday night training classes, weekend retreats and sermon series are just a few ways that this can be accomplished.

Here are some topics that I think need to be addressed often: family issues including marriage and parenting, singleness, service, personal financial management, spiritual disciplines, outreach, spiritual gifts, and Bible study. If you are investing in these areas in people's lives, I can guarantee that people will be growing. Maybe you just need to be more intentional than you have been in the past, and you need to be involving more people in the process. People grow when people are invested in.

You may not be able to do all of these, but if you added one additional class, sermon series or retreat that made you feel like your people would be better people at the end of that year, I think that would be a real success. Maybe you don't have the number of staff of a megachurch or the smooth presentation, but your people are growing, and it doesn't get any better than that.

CHURCH DEVELOPMENT AREA #7 —

Outreach

How do you proclaim Christ and help the needy in your community and the world? What training or activity is your church involved in that will orient people to world missions and personal evangelism? If your church were to disappear tomorrow, who outside of your own congregation would feel the impact?

<u>Care Connection</u> — Our church had a problem in this area, especially as it related to our local region. We were based in a rural area, and it was very difficult to identify people in need. Unlike the city, we didn't have a homeless population or a lot of obvious needs. We struggled with this for years, wanting to do something but somehow never able to find the right expression.

Finally, I was able to hear God's strategy. A big need was in our nearby city of Rochester, NY. It was only 20 miles from us, but in many ways, it was another world. A group of people in our church formed and focused specifically on connecting us with existing ministry opportunities in Rochester, where we could send teams to help. We called this outreach ministry the Care Connection. We formed a Ronald McDonald House team who went one night a month to prepare a meal for the folks staying at that house. We had a food bank team who went and helped distribute food on a weekly basis. We had an Open Door Mission team who went and helped serve the homeless there. We also developed a nursing home team. None of these ministries required us to start anything; our job was to help bridge the gap by providing volunteers for ministries that already existed.

Never underestimate the impact on the life of a person who goes for the first time to help at the Open Door Mission. Your small church might not be able to motivate a crowd or have several of these teams, but could you try just one for a season and see what impact it has?

<u>Annual Missions Sermon Series</u> — Every year we would dedicate a month in our church to teach on world missions. During this month, we taught biblically on the idea of why Christ followers should have passion for reaching the whole world for Christ. We would educate people on the spiritual conditions of different areas of the world. We would invite missionaries, who had dedicated their lives to reaching other parts of the world, to come speak to us about their burden. We would challenge people to give, above and beyond their tithes, to the spiritual and physical needs of different parts of the world. We would organize short-term trips to various places in the world, where people could do practical ministry like helping to build a church or showing the Jesus film in a primitive area in the language of the people there.

If we had not done this, where else would our congregation have heard educational and inspirational messages about caring for parts of the world that have no church or are facing devastating physical needs? Where would they have been challenged to take a portion of their income and give to the great cause of bringing the Gospel of Jesus to every part of the world? If you don't teach about this, your people may never have a chance to participate in this great cause. God puts in every church people who are burdened for outreach. Your job is to find them and help them organize in such a way that they can encourage others to join them.

<u>Special Invite Events</u> — You might consider including an annual personal evangelism sermon series or class, followed by an organized community outreach event. Great power can be released in a church by focusing things down to an event. For example, our youth ministry would focus on organizing an occasional Invite Night, where they would have a special fun event with prizes, and they might get 30 visitors. Ideally, we wanted them to invite their friends to every weekly youth group meeting, but there is something about focusing on special events that gets people excited. We would do a similar thing on occasional Sunday mornings called Friendship Day.

Now I can't control who comes to my church. And I don't need to focus my sense of success around how many people are added to our church's attendance. But shouldn't I feel a certain sense of success in that we pulled off two invite events this year, when we had done none for the last few years? Who might actually come is up to God, but whether we invite someone is up to us. Let's break free from the fear of rejection and instead focus on our doing what we have been asked to do, which is to invite people into a relationship with God. Let's take responsibility for what we can control and measure our success on whether we did what we were asked.

CHURCH DEVELOPMENT AREA #8 —

Spiritual Encounter

How are you leading people into deeper spiritual encounters with God? How are people being systematically led into the Baptism of the Holy Spirit? Where do people get to learn about the power gifts? When do they get to practice power gifts? How are their gifts stirred up in them?

<u>Baptism of the Holy Spirit Seminar</u> — I pastored a charismatic church that had a strong emphasis on spiritual encounter, and yet I came to realize that I had no systematic way to lead people into a spiritual encounter with God. In our tradition, the Baptism of the Holy Spirit is the doorway experience for people to enter into all of the power gifts, but the only opportunity a person had to be led into that experience was if I taught on it in a Sunday morning service. This happened rarely, so the church might have several years with no emphasis on this life-giving experience. I could sense the spiritual temperature of the church going down but was frustrated in how to confront this.

Finally, the insight came, and we instituted a two-hour seminar that I would do on a Sunday night every 3 months. The lid was lifted off of our church as all the interested people would come to be introduced into an encounter with the Holy Spirit with a release in the gift of spiritual language. Other churches even began sending people to our quarterly seminar. Now quarterly may be too often for you, but might you be able to offer something like this at least annually?

While you're thinking about this, let me ask you: How often do you give people a chance to receive Jesus Christ as their personal Savior? When was the last time you took a few moments at the end of a service to offer people a chance to receive Christ? Were you stopped by the fear that no one would respond? You can't control who will respond, but you can control if people have an opportunity to respond. Wouldn't it be a win if you could say we gave people 5 more chances to give their lives to Christ in our services this year than we did in all of last year? I call that success!

Ministry Team Development for Healing, Prophecy and Release — One of the turning points in the church I pastored was when several laymen in the church came to me and shared that they wanted to be involved in forming ministry teams that could minister to our congregation each Sunday in three areas. Healing — by this they meant physical healing primarily; if a person had any kind of disease, they wanted to be able to lay hands on them and minister to them. Prophecy — by this they meant personal words that reflected what the team felt God was saying personally to that person at that very moment. Release — by this they meant to pray against demonic oppression in people's lives and pray for emotional healing where it seemed needed.

Now prior to this, some of the elders and I would pray with people at the end of the service. But these people were proposing that the teams would receive pastor-approved training in each of the three areas they specialized in, and that the team members would then be held accountable for what they did and said. For example, in the case of the personal prophecy, every word was recorded, so that if there was any controversy, the word could be judged by the leaders of the church.

Fortunately, controversy was not what happened. Instead, each Sunday four trained teams — Salvation, Healing, Prophecy and Release — would line up front at the end of the service and be available to minister to people personally. These teams would often stay and pray with people for an hour or more after the formal service had ended. So many powerful things happened. The amount of ministry that went forth on Sunday mornings greatly increased, with no additional burden added to me as the pastor, as I was not on any of these teams — although I was always welcome to participate and observe.

Now our church didn't necessarily grow numerically from this, but our ministry to people exploded in impact. People would come to us from other churches if they had a special need, because they knew that every week, no matter what I spoke on, these teams would be available to minister to people's needs. This is a beautiful illustration of the kind of improvements your church can experience, no matter what is going on in the offering plate.

Prophetic Presbytery Weekend — These were times when we would invite people who had a proven gift of prophecy to come visit with our church and minister to those whom we had previously identified as needing a special word from the Lord. These words were not in competition with the Bible, nor were they held on the same level; these were words that drew upon the Bible and were applied to the lives of those who were being ministered to. Part of what made it so spiritually moving is that the people speaking did not know those they were ministering to, and yet what they said was so relevant to what those people were going through. It was a very moving experience that would stir people in their spiritual lives and often release fresh motivation to pursue the Lord.

Other ways people could be inspired to have a fresh spiritual encounter might include spiritual growth weekends, classes on power gifts and how to use them, and annual sermon series on how the Spirit works in the life of the believer.

CHURCH DEVELOPMENT AREA #9 —

Leadership Development

This process answers the question, "How do you develop leaders in the church?"

Of course, the first step in developing other leaders in the church is to develop yourself as a leader. One of the most powerful tools that can help you in this is developing the tools for getting your own life together. I call this a Personal Growth Plan. This is a tool to help you identify what are the most important things that you are called to focus on in a given year and then how to work those objectives into your calendar. I will be working on a version to share with you on my website (notmanyfathers. com), but you don't have to wait for me to get started. Some other books that can help you with this process are *First Things First* by Stephen Covey and *Living Forward* by Michael Hyatt. Let me also encourage you to consider taking a Zoom class with me, where I can train you personally in personal growth and pastoral skills like preaching and leadership thinking.

Web Resources — There are amazing Christian leadership materials on websites like YouTube. If you gather resources, you can put together a YouTube Academy for the key leaders in your church, without you having to personally create a single thing. You can put together a list of resources, that people can watch and then discuss with you, that would have an amazing impact on the growth of the key people you want to develop for leadership.

Mentor Groups — One of the best moves I ever made was to start meeting every Saturday morning for 2 hours with 12 potential leaders (age 40 and under) who attended my church. I would meet with them for 18 months. Over and over again, I can point to members of these groups who have gone on to make a meaningful impact in the kingdom of God. Several became pastors, several are elders in churches, and almost all are influencers in their churches.

The schedule would include 15 minutes of fellowship, followed by 15 minutes of worship led by alternating members of the group. I would then teach for 30 minutes. Then we would have an accountability discussion for an hour, led by alternating members of the group, where they would discuss things they were struggling with in their lives, often related to issues I had taught on in previous weeks. We would each share our struggles in the same area, and if we had found some victory, we would share things that had helped.

Some of the topics I taught on over the 18 months included marriage and family issues, battling pornography, developing personal growth plans, general leadership issues, personal financial management, and how to preach. These were all things that I had taught in the church over the years, so it didn't require much extra work for me; it just took time to be with them. Without question, this was some of the most productive time I've ever spent in ministry.

Leadership Skill Classes — After pastoring for 20 years, one of the things I realized was that many of the values I had communicated at the beginning of the church were not being retaught to the next generation of leaders who were coming up. So we created a class called Doorway to Influence. The purpose of the class was to give next generation leaders the rationale behind some of the decisions that the leadership had made in the past. This included answering questions like why showing up to church is important, why we need to be very careful in our relationships with the opposite sex, why do we tithe, why water baptism is important, why the Baptism in the Holy Spirit means so much to us, and other issues. You need to have a way that your new leaders can make the commitments that your early leaders made.

CHURCH DEVELOPMENT AREA #10 —

Strategic Planning

How do you evaluate and improve your church? How do you set vision and build toward that vision?

Strategic planning sounds very complicated, but the truth is that in our lives we strategically plan all the time without even realizing it has a name. Strategic planning begins by identifying the preferred future.

For example, if it were a trip it would look like this: Where do we want to go? We want to go to Kalamazoo, Michigan, to visit my son and his family there; that is the preferred upcoming future. The next question is: How do we get there in the most efficient, safe, and cost-effective way? Will our car make the trip, or should we rent a car? Would flying be better use of our time? Do we want to insert some days of vacation in around the trip and visit some sites on the way there? Do we have to alter our trip because of obstacles? (For example, the route through Canada is temporarily closed due to Covid-19 shutdown.) Other questions include: What do we need to bring to make the trip enjoyable? Should we bring any gifts for the grandkids? When will we arrive and when will we leave? Are there any things that must be done while we are there? How much will the whole trip cost? Do we have enough money to pay for the trip? This is strategic planning.

One of the best things that can happen as you are guiding your church is to establish a strategic planning group. It could be your board, or the elders, or a committee that is formed specifically for that purpose. The key is that even if the process starts with a small group, you eventually involve as many people in the process as possible. Involvement encourages ownership and commitment to the vision.

So, the group begins by asking the question: Where are we going as a church? Or to say it another way: If God had His perfect way with our church, what would it look like? I express it as, "What would it look like?" because that is exactly what you're trying to do — to see a picture, a vision of what the desired future is supposed to be.

This picture is very powerful. You have heard the expression that a picture is worth a thousand words. It is true. If you can paint a compelling picture of the God-ordained future, it will touch people's hearts like nothing else. What you're looking for is a picture, not an explanation. An explanation clarifies; a vision inspires. An explanation touches the mind; a vision touches the heart and spirits of everyone who sees it.

What would your church look like if God has His perfect way there? Do you see people with their hands raised and tears flowing down their cheeks as they sing worship to the Lord? Do you see married couples humbling themselves and begging for help as they try to not lose their marriage and family? Do you see the church filled every night with support groups sitting in circles, helping people get released from addictions and bondages through humble prayer and mutual confession? Do you see children responding to God's Word as teachers challenge them to surrender their whole lives to Jesus Christ? Are those children filled with confidence as they learn how to look in the Bible for themselves? Do you see ambulances pulling up to the church to bring in the sick to be healed? Do you see cars lined up around the block to receive free food from your food distribution center? Do you see the altar of the church filled with people crying tears of surrender as they say yes to God's call to the mission field? Do you see 10% of your youth choosing some form of ministry as a vocation? Do you see the church filled with people from all races and ethnic groups embracing one another and supporting each other?

The answers to these questions are going to be different for every church, because your vision will be unique to your team and your community as the resources and gifts are different for every group. The key is that you begin to form a picture of what your church is meant to be, and then you begin to lay out the steps that you feel will get you from where you are now to where you are supposed to be. Of course, there is always a gap between where you are and the vision you see.

Strategic planning is simply your group answering the question, "What one thing could we work on now that would move us one step closer to where we feel we should be?" It could be as simple as repainting the entryway of the church or doing research on how a food bank can be set up. After you successfully do that one thing, you ask the question again and then do the next thing that is going to move you in the direction of the vision you see. Each one of these small victories should be celebrated, and soon you will have a string of them, which turns into momentum — and before you know it, that area of the church begins to look like your vision. Then you look at another area and do the same thing.

This is victory for the small church. This is what success looks like: becoming the vision God has given your church. It is not measured against any other church; it is absolutely unique to you, because only you have the unique hand you have been dealt of resources, people, gifts and calling.

You and your people will become passionate about your vision. You will be perpetually motivated by the picture of the future you see. You will have plenty to celebrate as you slowly move just one step closer to what God has called you to be.

Final Thoughts

There's an old adage that has helped me over the years at various times in my ministry: "Begun is half done!" I have found repeatedly in life that overcoming the initial inertia often caused by perfectionism and the fear of failure is critical to ever experiencing accomplishment and the confidence that comes with it.

One of the great strongholds that keeps us from fulfilling our destiny is paralyzing perfectionism — or to say it another way: the fear of failure. We are each so aware of all the ways we have disappointed ourselves by not perfectly accomplishing what we have attempted that we start to doubt that we are capable of doing anything right. We don't understand that God is more interested in the process of our struggle and what it builds in us than He is in any perfect accomplishments that we might have. If God wanted perfect accomplishments, He could have that at any moment; remember, He is all powerful. What He wants is the byproduct of our attempting to dare great things for Him. That byproduct is the maturity, humility, and faith that forms in us as we risk following His call. Any accomplishment that we achieve is only temporary, but what is formed in us is eternal.

If we don't understand the ways of God, we can interpret that we face resistance and experience failure as signs that God is not with us or that we are somehow inherently flawed and disqualified from being on God's A-team. Nothing could be further from the truth! God is not bound by our efficiency, because He is all powerful. God draws tremendous pleasure from our efforts to please Him.

And the fact that He decided to invest you into a small church or ministry says nothing about your ability — and everything about His extravagant love for the people you are serving. Sometimes He places incredibly capable people in small communities — not because they are incapable of anything else, but because He deeply loves that community and He wants them to experience His extravagant love.

You may feel inadequate to the challenges I've given you in this book, but your inadequacy is the price tag for the growth that God wants to occur in you. You must dare, you must try, you must attempt — or nothing good can happen. You don't have to be perfect; you just need to be fighting for what you understand God wants to do through your ministry and that reaching for His highest and best will deeply change you and please the heart of God.

There is an amazing truth that is often overlooked: Not everyone who swings the bat hits the ball every time, but if you don't swing, you will never hit it — guaranteed!

A friend once sent me this article from the Associated Press about a little girl who performed one of the most difficult plays in baseball, an unassisted triple play. The headline read *"Girl Proves Adage: No Pain, No Gain."*

"Richmond, VA – It wasn't the nicest experience, but Jessica Lafferty's reward for her pain was an unassisted triple play.

Jessica, 7, was playing shortstop for the Maroon team Thursday against the Royal Blues. With the runners on first and second, a Royal Blue batter hit a sharp line drive that struck Jessica in the chest. Jessica doubled over in pain but pinned the ball against her body for the first out.

Hurt, Jessica stumbled toward her coaches, who were standing at second base. In the process, she recorded the second out by bumping into the Royal Blue runner who had strayed off second base. Jessica, still cradling the ball and in obvious pain, reached second, where she found the Royal Blue runner who had been on first, and who had not tagged up. Jessica ran into him for the third out.

Jessica, flashing an occasional smile between sniffles, was able to stay in the game."

Jessica experienced a simple truth: If you're on the field, anything can happen. But if you don't get on the field, even God can't do a miracle for you.

Now you may not understand anything about baseball, but you must understand this: The awareness of our weaknesses and imperfections is the foundation for being used by God. "But we have this treasure in jars of clay to show that this all-surpassing power is from God and not from us." (2 Corinthians 4:7 NIV) God puts His glory in frail, flaw-filled human beings, because when God uses you, it shows that the power is coming from Him.

You thought your weaknesses, imperfections and failures disqualified you from being used by God, but God says these are the very things that qualify you to experience His miracle power flowing through you to the ministry you lead.

"Brothers, think of what you were when you were called. Not many of you were wise by human standards; not many were influential; not many were of noble birth. But God chose the foolish things of the world to shame the wise; God chose the weak things of the world to shame the strong. He chose the lowly things of this world and the despised things — and the things that are not — to nullify the things that are, so that no one may boast before him. It is because of him that you are in Christ Jesus, who has become for us wisdom from God — that is, our righteousness, holiness, and redemption. Therefore, as it is written: 'Let him who boasts boast in the Lord.'" (1 Corinthians 1:26-31 NIV)

Pastor, you may feel small, weak, and unable to successfully accomplish what God is calling you to do. But let me assure you that if you define success in your church the way God does, His miracle power will divinely enable you to fulfill your mission. You will bring Him pleasure and you will hear the words, "Well done, My good and faithful servant."

Resources

What is NOT MANY FATHERS about?

Many emerging Christian leaders have come into spiritual leadership with little experience or practical ministry training. In many cases, their home life had little spiritual grounding, and their formal training was secular. Yet they have had a powerful encounter with God and feel called to serve Him. Their call is real, but success is not guaranteed.

Now they need relationship with someone who has more ministry experience — a spiritual father to share experience, critical skills and inspiration for the mission they are facing. A mentor with a history of ministry experience and the heart of a spiritual father giving support during a leader's formative stages can greatly increase the possibility of a long-lasting and effective ministry.

> *For though you have countless guides in Christ, you do not have many fathers.* 1 Corinthians 4:15

Paul says in 1 Corinthians 4:15: "For though you have countless guides in Christ, you do not have many fathers." The mission of Not Many Fathers is to impart to others what God has given me and other spiritual fathers, encouraging them to accomplish more than we ever have — to help emerging Christian leaders in how to make wise life and leadership decisions, to preach dynamically, and to boldly launch their ministry visions so they can reach their God-given potential.

The tools we use to accomplish this are writing inspirational leadership development books that can be consumed in about an hour, and speaking in churches and conferences, along with classes, discipleship, and personal consulting that are done in person and online.

More resources from Mike Cavanaugh

Are you interested in reading more of Mike Cavanaugh's ministry-related books? Other titles include: *How to Not Quit Your Ministry* and *How to Lead Your Ministry through Change*. All of these are available in ebook format at notmanyfathers.com or as printed books on Amazon.

No one starts out knowing everything they need to succeed. If you're not satisfied with what is happening in your ministry, these resources might be exactly what you need to strengthen the impact of God's calling in your life. Check out **notmanyfathers.com**. You can contact Mike at mike@notmanyfathers.com.

How to support this ministry

When people hear what Not Many Fathers is attempting to do, they often want to contribute to support the vision. Mike does not draw a salary, and all the expenses of the ministry are covered by Mike's traveling to speak, tuition from some classes he teaches, and the personal donations of people who want to invest in the vision or to say thank you for the free resources they have received.

If you're interested in giving financially, you can go to the website notmanyfathers.com and donate (donations are not tax-deductible). If you would like to give a larger gift and need a tax deductible receipt, please contact Mike at mike@notmanyfathers.com; he has tax exempt organizations associated with him that can provide a receipt for you.

If your church would like to support Not Many Fathers as part of its missions giving, Mike would be happy to meet with your board to explain the mission and thank them personally. The expenses of maintaining the website and publishing are real, and your help would be greatly appreciated.

Dedication

Throughout my adult life, there has been one person who has stood beside me in everything I have attempted and has given her all to support me in every behind-the-scene way possible. She is my wife, Terri. There is no ministry that I have given myself to that my wife has not made possible by working with me. Sometimes her work has been acknowledged with pay, and other times she has just done what needed to be done with no thought of herself. No ministry I've led would have succeeded without her personal sacrifice. I have often received the applause that she has deserved. At this season of my life, I feel nothing but overwhelming gratitude and love every time I look at her. What a fantastic partner she has been. In this series of books to help beginning ministers, she is my editor, layout and design person. I dedicate this whole series to her, and I thank God for every day that we can continue to partner together in life and ministry.

Mike Cavanaugh is the founder and director of Not Many Fathers, a ministry dedicated to mentoring emerging Christian leaders in how to make wise decisions, preach dynamically, and boldly initiate their visions so they can reach their God-given potential.

Mike was the founder and director of BASIC College Ministry, which after 40 years is still helping churches impact students for Christ. He also founded and directed Mobilized to Serve, which challenged single adults to serve Christ. During this time, he also wrote the book *God's Call to the Single Adult,* which has sold over 100,000 copies and is still published today under the title *The Power and Purpose of Singleness.*

Mike pastored Elim Gospel Church, a dynamic congregation of nearly 1,000 in Lima, NY, for 20 years, including leading them to raise the funds and construct a 60,000 sq.ft. ministry center. He has also served as the vice president of Elim Fellowship, a ministerial organization where he worked with hundreds of pastors, missionaries and Christian leaders.

Most recently, Mike served for 8 years as the president of Elim Bible Institute and College, where he led the school to achieve full accreditation and saw hundreds of thousands of dollars of aid released for students at the only accredited charismatic Bible college in New York.

He is a graduate of Elim Bible Institute and College, Roberts Wesleyan College, and Bakke Graduate University. Mike and his wife, Terri, reside in Lima, NY, and have three adult children and nine grandchildren.

CPSIA information can be obtained
at www.ICGtesting.com
Printed in the USA
LVHW050223121121
702954LV00007B/50

9 781945 423321